GET YOU!

TINA BLACK

BE A LEADER

22 21 20 19 18 17   8 7 6 5 4 3 2 1

BE A LEADER — Get Your Leadership On!
©2017 Tina Black

All rights reserved. Except as permitted under the U.S. Copyright Act of 1976, no part of this publication may be reproduced, distributed, or transmitted in any form or by any means, or stored in a database or retrieval system, without the prior written permission of the publisher.

TULSA, OKLAHOMA

Published by:
Emerge Publishing, LLC
9521B Riverside Parkway, Suite 243
Tulsa, Oklahoma 74137
Phone: 888.407.4447
www.EmergePublishing.com

ISBN: 978-1-943127-51-1 Paperback
ISBN: 978-1-943127-52-8 Digital/E-book

BISAC Category:
BUS071000 BUSINESS & ECONOMICS / Leadership
SEL027000 SELF-HELP / Personal Growth / Success

Author Contact:
Tina Black
2950 Lapeer Road
Port Huron, MI 48060
Tel: 810.987.8118
Email: tina@tinablack.com
Web: www.tinablack.net

ATTENTION: ORGANIZATIONS and CORPORATIONS
Bulk quantity discounts for reselling, gifts, or fundraising are available. For more information, please contact Tina@tinablack.net.

20% of the proceeds from this book will go to the nonprofit Andrew Gomez Dream Foundation, which provides educational support to cosmetology students and graduates and partners annually with other select charities to jointly raise funds.

Printed in the United States of America.

DEDICATION

I dedicate this book to my staff. Without each and every one of you (and even those no longer in our company), I would not be who I am today. I am grateful for all of you.

ACKNOWLEDGEMENTS

John Maxwell, for opening my eyes to see the importance of leadership training and constant personal growth.

My husband Bryan and our children, Brianna and Justin, for showing me that leadership starts at home.

My mom and dad, for always teaching me integrity.

My partners, Winn Claybaugh and John Paul DeJoria, for showing me an example of true leaders.

FOREWORD

By Paul Martinelli
President, the John Maxwell Team

I've worked with Tina Black since she joined the John Maxwell Team in 2012. I've had the privilege of seeing her leadership in action and observing her nonstop commitment to growth, both as a leader and as a human being. Tina quickly became one of our biggest cheerleaders, referring numerous people to the team as she eagerly shared what she'd learned as part of the team and the way it impacted her life. Tina's book, *Be a Leader*, reflects her passion for helping people by sharing what she knows. With a watchful observer's eye, she is constantly on the lookout for new lessons to spark her growth—and she eagerly shares what she finds! I love her *Be a Leader* messages and its user-friendly format. As someone who teaches authentic journaling, I know the power it has to engage your consciousness and transform your life. Leadership doesn't just happen: it takes time, tools, and commitment. If you set aside the time, use the tools in this book, and commit to your growth as a leader, you will surely reach your goal.

PEOPLE ARE TALKING ABOUT *BE A LEADER!*

"Tina Black is an amazing human being. Her book, *Be a Leader: Get Your Leadership On!* is a must read. Full of wonderful insights, terrific stories, and gems of wisdom on leadership and life. Highly recommended!"

— **Charles Marcus**
Motivational Speaker
Best-Selling Author of *Success Is Not a Spectator Sport*

"The biggest challenge for many of us is implementing the things we know we should be doing. Living with intention and holding ourselves to a higher standard is not always easy, but if you read Tina's book, and work through and engage with the exercises week by week, you will be taken on a journey of self-improvement that will bring about positive change in your life, your business, and the lives of those around you."

— **Antony Whitaker**
Hairdresser, Coach, Author, and Speaker

"I have read *Be a Leader* by Tina Black and I highly recommend it to anyone who wants thoughtful and intelligent wisdom related to leadership. Page after page is full of solid suggestions into so many areas, with a focus on personal accountability and teamwork. Tina takes her lessons learned from her personal experiences in Africa and other places, and her time spent with a number of outstanding leaders, and gives the reader great insight and knowledge that can be applied to whatever level of leadership applies to you. Well done, Tina, and thank you for all you have given us."

— **Luke Jacobellis**
President, John Paul Mitchell Systems

TRANSFORMATION BEGINS IN ME

I know I need to constantly get my leadership on, and the way I do that is to always have a growth plan. One of the best ways to grow your leadership is through questions. Questions that propel you to action. Questions to move you forward. That's why I've written this leadership journal: to get you thinking about the next steps that you, too, need to take to get your leadership on.

* * * * *

I'll never forget that phone call as long as I live. It was in June 2012, the day I returned from Guatemala with the John Maxwell Team. I was one of 150 John Maxwell coaches and speakers who had traveled with John to teach leadership principles to Guatemalan leaders for a week, to help transform their nation. You see, John realized a long time ago that everything rises and falls on leadership.

Years ago, God had called me into short-term missions, and for years I struggled with what God meant by that calling. I had gone on mission trips to Mexico, Haiti, and recently to Africa, but I knew I had to do more. Going on the Guatemala trip finally answered my questions, and I knew it would be the first of many trips I would take with the John Maxwell Team. Like John, I realized that, yes, I want to help the helpless and will continue to do mission trips, but I also realized that real transformation won't happen in these countries without transformed leaders. Anything else is like putting a Band-Aid on a gushing wound. Thank God for John's vision!

That week in Guatemala, we taught a lesson titled "Transformation Begins in Me." I taught police department leaders, then schoolteachers, and finally military cadets. On the last day, tears streamed down my face as I realized I would never be able to incite change in my family, my spouse, my staff, or my business until I transformed. I was the problem. No one else.

When I got home that June day in 2012, I scheduled a conference call with my team leaders. As tears streamed down my face, I apologized for being such a horrible leader. I promised that I would be better. I vowed to change my ways and invest in them.

We all laugh about it now and we call it "old Tina vs. new Tina." I was transformed, and I continue to be transformed. I'm not where I want to be but I'm definitely not where I was!

Four years later, I've seen more growth and more change in my business than ever before. It's true—when you invest in your own growth, everyone around you automatically grows. John Maxwell calls it the Law of the Lid: each one of us holds the potential (the lid) for everyone around us. Wow, is that an awesome responsibility! It can either empower us or overwhelm us.

I hope you choose the former: I hope this message and this book will empower you.

Over the past 4 years my personal mantra has become, "Don't be obsessed with money, or success, or whatever it is, but rather be obsessed with improvement." A few years ago I started my own leadership blog at www.tinablack.net; this book includes many of my past leadership messages, along with some new ones so you can start your growth journey like I did 4 years ago.

Over the next 52 weeks, I hope to make it easy for you to grow and be obsessed with improvement, as I call it. In just 10 minutes a week, you can transform yourself and watch as the people around you suddenly transform. In fact, this will be so simple that you'll want to grab one of those old Staples buttons, press it, and yell, "That was easy!"

Before you start this book, do what I did 4 years ago in Guatemala: point your right finger up high and say (in Spanish), *Transformacion esté en me!* It means, "Transformation will be in me!" And when you say "me," point your finger at your heart.

Let the transformation begin, and together let's get our leadership on!

Be a leader!

Transform Yourself in 52 Weeks!

BE A LEADER

Week

No One Ever Succeeds Alone

"No one ever succeeds alone."

— Darren Hardy

Darren Hardy, the publisher of *Success* magazine and one of my biggest mentors and leadership gurus, reminds us that *no one ever succeeds alone.*

All of my mentors have taught me this. I'll never forget the moment when my partner and number-one mentor Winn Claybaugh led his Shot-in-the-Arm motivational class for all of the Paul Mitchell school owners; that was the day my eyes completely opened to the fact that I need people to help me succeed. Until then, I had lived almost my entire life thinking, *I don't need anybody. I can do this all by myself.* Even though I had played team sports my whole life, I had never truly gotten the message that no one ever succeeds alone.

I hear similar statements from my staff and students all the time: "I don't need anybody." "I don't care if no one likes me." "I'm going to keep to myself from now on."

Can I just tell you that this is a very dangerous place to be? How do I know? Because I tried it for many years and I was not able to succeed in life or my business. I wasted a ton of years spinning my wheels.

Listen—no one ever succeeds alone. Stop making it all about you.

Some days when I'm not connected to God, I, too, make it all about me. I have pity parties. I whine. I complain.

So here's my challenge this week to myself and to you: stop thinking or saying statements like, "I don't care what anyone thinks," or "I don't need anyone; I can do it myself."

Stop. Just stop. Instead, ask, "Who do I know who can help me?"

Trust me, when you really unlock your selfish behavior, someone surfaces. Join a church youth group. A Bible study. The Chamber of Commerce. Toastmasters. One of my Mastermind groups!

You've got this! I know you want this.

Remember, no one ever succeeds alone.

TINA BLACK

What do you want to accomplish today? This week? This year?

Who can you enlist to help you?

What community group can you join to network more with like-minded people?

Week 2

Forget Self-confidence: Ask for "God-fidence"

"We have been taught that all people have a basic need to believe in themselves. However, that is a misconception ... We do not need self-confidence; we need God-confidence!"

— JOYCE MEYER

One day, I read such a great message from Christian author and speaker Joyce Meyer that I couldn't wait to share parts of it. In her Daily Devotionals, Joyce wrote, "Everyone talks about self-confidence .... We have been taught that all people have a basic need to believe in themselves. However, that is a misconception ... We do not need self-confidence; we need God-confidence!" Joyce went on to warn us never to give credit to ourselves but always to give the credit to God.

The world constantly tells us we need more self-confidence, but God tells us that's a dangerous place to be. Yes, we need confidence, but we need God-confidence. (I like to call it *God-fidence*.)

I have struggled with low self-esteem my entire life, but ever since I have been closer to God and my walk with Jesus, I am more confident in my skin. Now I am thankful for my low self-esteem because I honestly believe that if I'd had high confidence I would have walked around with a high ego and never leaned on God for confidence.

Be careful not to focus so much on yourself that you become selfish and develop an "it's all about me" attitude. Do you know anyone who gossips, constantly acts like a victim, complains of everyone wronging them, has a constant negative attitude, resists all systems or rules at work, or has an "it's not fair" attitude? Look in the mirror—I hope it's not you! Honestly, I look in the mirror daily and ask myself if I have any of these attitudes. When I do (because, yes, I do), I ask God to take them from me.

Listen, it's easy. It really is! All you have to do is hang out with visionaries who think this way, and they will rub off on you. Come on, now. Don't tell me you don't have anyone. You have me. You have God. Have you ever heard the quote, "Let go and let God"? Honestly, God's not impressed with your titles, your house, your money, the kind of car you drive, or the trophies on your wall; he's impressed with your heart. By the way, "Examine Your Heart" is a chapter in my first book, *Be Amazing*.

If you knew you only had a month to live, which five characteristics would you change about yourself? Go ahead; write them down. What are you waiting for?

Forget self-confidence. Get God-fidence!

TINA BLACK

Do you struggle with self-confidence? Do you have an "It's all about me" attitude? Do you gossip, play victim, blame others, be negative? Do you resist systems at school, home, or work? Do you often hear yourself say, "It's not fair"?

Examine your heart. What five characteristics will you change about yourself?

BE A LEADER

Week 3

Forget New Year's Resolutions: Choose One Word

"Words are, of course, the most powerful drug used by mankind."

— RUDYARD KIPLING

I wanted to share with you a personal habit that I started using years ago. It was inspired by author and speaker Jon Gordon and his book, *One Word That Will Change Your Life*. Jon challenges readers with the following idea: instead of making a New Year's resolution, he asks us to choose a word for the year—and not just a *good* word but a *God* word.

Check out Jon Gordon's "One Word Will Change Your Life" video: https://www.youtube.com/watch?v=CShvhZ7D0fg

In the past few years, my words have been *love, patience, listen,* and *uncommon.*

Each year, I take time to dig deep and find my God word by asking myself these questions:

What do I need to stop doing?

What do I need start doing?

What do I need to do more of?

What do I need to do less of?

By the way, an article in *Forbes* magazine pointed out that only 8 percent of New Year's resolutions actually come to fruition for people (http://onforb.es/J13duI). So here's my challenge to myself and to you: instead of wasting time on resolutions that rarely make it past January, let's find our God words for the coming year!

TINA BLACK

What's your word for this year? How are you going to live it out?

Don't have one? Then ask yourself these questions:

What do I need to stop doing?

What do I need to start doing?

What do I need to do more of?

What do I need to do less of?

BE A LEADER

Week 4

Live an Uncommon Life

"Successful people do all the things unsuccessful people won't do."

— JOHN PAUL DEJORIA

Last week I challenged you to come up with one word for the year. Have you thought of your word yet?

In 2016, my word came to me while I was in church. The pastor was talking about being uncommon, and I immediately knew that was my word for the year. Then I heard a message from my mentor Darren Hardy, best-selling author of *The Entrepreneur Roller Coaster* and *The Compound Effect*. Darren talked about being careful to not be complacent and referred to complacency as the destroyer of success. After hearing that, I knew for sure I was on the right path with my word.

Uncommon people have the power to change the world!

Uncommon people are not complacent. Uncommon people embrace change. Uncommon people do all the things that unsuccessful people won't do. Uncommon people get up early in the morning and work on self-improvement. Uncommon people work out every day and eat healthy. Uncommon people make sure they stay ahead of the game and become the number-one employees in their businesses. Uncommon people keep score. Uncommon people live "wholly" lives: they stay balanced professionally, physically, intellectually, emotionally, and spiritually.

In his video series on how to be successful, salon owner and stylist Kelly Cardenas, another one of my mentors, says that successful people have to be "certifiably insane." Although his word selection should not be taken literally, it truly drives the point that to be successful you have to be uncommon.

TINA BLACK

Are you common or uncommon? How do you know?

Are you complacent?

Do you embrace change?

Do you do things that unsuccessful people won't do?

Do you get up early in the morning and work on self-improvement?

Do you work out every day and eat healthy foods?

Do you make sure you stay ahead of the game to become the number-one employee in your business?

Do you keep score?

Do you live a "wholly" life: do you stay balanced professionally, physically, intellectually, emotionally, and spiritually?

Week

Understand Your Value

*"If you put a small value on yourself, rest assured,
the world will not raise the price."*

– JOHN C. MAXWELL, THE 15 INVALUABLE LAWS OF GROWTH

In my book *Be Amazing*, one of my seven steps to success is "Understand Your Value." That concept also appears in John Maxwell's book, *The 15 Invaluable Laws of Growth*, especially in the chapter titled "The Law of the Mirror," in which he says, "If you put a small value on yourself, rest assured, the world will not raise the price."

Can you believe that no two thumbprints are the same? It's hard to imagine, with over 7 billion people in the world at any given time, but it's true. You are unique. There is no one like you!

I have struggled most of my life to truly grasp the idea that I am valuable or "more precious than rubies," as the Bible says. I doubt if I'll ever graduate from this, but one thing I know is that God tells us we were "made in his image." So I will constantly look in the mirror and, even on the days I don't feel like it, I will remind myself that I am valuable.

How about you? Do you, too, struggle with this? Do you ever "cut yourself down" to others? Do you sometimes walk out of the house not looking your best? Do you sometimes overeat and sometimes skip your workouts? These are all signs that we don't value ourselves.

When we have our brand-new babies, what do we do? We dress them up in the best clothes; we make sure everyone sees that our children are valuable, right?

What about your cat or dog? We love our pets so much that we give them the best food, the best of everything. Yet we look at ourselves and say, "Nah, you're not valuable. Go ahead and put that unhealthy food in your body. Nah, you don't need to dress your best, you're not worth it." Is that you on any given day? Yeah, I get it. It's me, too! This is a constant struggle of mine.

So here's my challenge to you. Understand your value! Daily renew your mind. Say your affirmation statements. Write on your mirror, "Hey, you sexy thing!" "Hey beautiful!" Or best yet, "I am valuable."

Go ahead—try it on this week.

TINA BLACK

What steps will you make today to love yourself? Choose a daily mantra or affirmation and write it here. Then write it on your mirror, and start saying it every day.

BE A LEADER

Week 6

Love the Challenges

"A strong woman looks a challenge dead in the eye and gives it a wink."

— GINA CAREY, SOUL SINGER

My challenge to you this week is to *love the challenges*.

I challenge myself a lot, and I can honestly say that I really love challenges. I love taking on new opportunities and pushing myself to hit my goals. In the past few years, I wrote my first book and became co-owner of a salon with my daughter Brianna. I joined the John Maxwell leadership, coaching, and speaking team, which required me to challenge myself to fine-tune my speaking skills by working with a speaking coach and turning in speaking videos each week. I also challenged myself to complete the six-week course and make the two-year commitment to become an ambassador for Bright Pink, a nonprofit organization dedicated to educating people about breast and ovarian cancer. This year, I set new challenges to finish this book and open new schools and salons.

How about you? Do you love your challenges? Are you willing to push yourself and take on some new ones? I personally find it energizing, especially when I take on challenges that fit my strengths.

So ... what new challenges are *you* willing to take on this year?

TINA BLACK

What challenges or struggles are you up against this week?

How can you push past them or use them to propel yourself forward?

What new challenges can you take on to complete this week? This month? This year?

BE A LEADER

Week

Love the Competition

"I play to win, whether during practice or a real game. And I will not let anything get in the way of me and my competitive enthusiasm to win."

— MICHAEL JORDAN

This week I want to challenge you to love the competition. At a recent John Maxwell coaching, speaking, and leadership team training event, John challenged us over and over to want to be first. He said no one ever gets noticed in second or third place. Desire to win! Push yourself to win!

Honestly, this has never been a challenge for me. I was brought up by an incredible father who encouraged competition in our family. Shoot, we would compete just running up the stairs on our way to bed. My dad challenged us with everything! Even when we were kids, he would challenge us to compete for a buck playing Yahtzee. I grew up playing games—bowling, board games, card games, you name it—and always trying to beat my brothers and sisters. I grew up running track and playing basketball and other sports, and always striving to win, always striving to be the best.

Competition is one of my strengths. I truly believe it makes me who I am today as a business leader. I want to win. I want to be the best. Just ask my team; they'll say, "Yep, with Tina it's always about being the best. She loves to win." My competitive spirit has motivated me to choose only the best players for my team. Without them I'd never win. They love competition, too, whether it's competing to raise the most during our FUNraising season or challenging our students to take part in retail competitions.

Push yourself. Strive to be the best. Be the first. Want to win. Don't settle for anything less!

Having trouble with this? Then surround yourself with competitors. Surround yourself with winners. Who's in your inner circle?

Love the competition!

TINA BLACK

Are you competitive? If not, which competitive people could you surround yourself with?

Week

"Some People You Need to Love from a Distance"

"Don't waste another minute dealing with a toxic, negative, energy-draining person. Some people are wired for negativity. They love being argumentative, combative, and abusive. Run for your life as quickly as possible."

— LES BROWN

Televangelist and author Joel Osteen shared an amazing message about choosing the right inner circle. He said, "There may be times when you just have to love people from a distance."

What does this mean for you? It means you need to be careful in choosing who you hang out with. Don't spend time with people who are always negative, always discouraged. If you're in a relationship with people who are always giving and never receiving, those people will drain you. That explains why so many people are worn out, stressed out, and frustrated: they're trying to keep people happy, feeling like they are responsible for making everyone happy. Listen: that's not your job. Stop being a doormat. Yes, you sometimes need to carry others but not constantly. It's easy to think you can do it all but you are cheating yourself. God wants to give you eagles in your life, but you're so busy hanging out with chickens—people sucking the life out of you—that you're not cultivating relationships that can carry you. Hang out with people who inspire you, motivate you, and cause you to rise higher.

Now you might be saying, "But Tina, those negative people you described, that's my family." Well, listen—sometimes you need to love people from a distance. You don't have to make a big announcement. Just spend less time with them.

Maybe you're asking, "But Tina, where are these eagles?" There are so many opportunities out there to find eagles: at church, volunteering with nonprofits, attending seminars, reading self-help books, etc. Why not join one of my Mastermind groups? Surround yourself with eagles.

My challenge to you this week is to evaluate your inner circle. Is there anyone you need to love from a distance?

TINA BLACK

Evaluate your inner circle. Write the names of the top five people you hang out with, and then rate them on a scale of 1–5, where 1 means they are always negative, and 5 means they are always positive.

Who can you start loving from a distance?

Who can you reach out to today, to help you find more eagles?

BE A LEADER

Week 9

Love Negative People

*"Negative people need drama like oxygen. Stay positive.
It will take their breath away."*

— TONY GASKINS

This week's challenge is to love negative people. I know you're saying, "What?!?!?" I've consistently asked you to be careful about who you hang out with and who you choose for your inner circle, and now suddenly I'm challenging you to love negative people?!?!?

Please notice that I'm not saying, "Surround yourself with negative people," or "Become a negative person." I'm challenging you to *love* negative people ... for several reasons:

- Noticing and loving negative people reminds you to have gratitude for your positive attitude.
- The negative people in your life are a gift you can appreciate. They stretch you to evaluate your convictions and challenge you to know why you believe something.
- You can add value and create magic for negative people and challenge them to be positive. (Most negative people are not even aware they are negative). Wow, what an impact you can make!
- Trust me, as an entrepreneur I've had my share of negative staff, clients, and students in my path, and I have not always loved them. In fact, this challenge is just as much for me as it is for you.

One day, I was eating at a restaurant when I noticed a very unhappy waitress. I made it a point to smile at her and encourage her, and by the end of my dining experience her demeanor was much better. *Boom! Success!* One more changed life!

I want to live my life knowing I've made a difference in the lives of others. So here's your challenge for this week: Notice the people around you. If you notice a negative person, do what you can verbally and nonverbally to positively influence him or her. See how you feel afterwards.

Now, go love negative people!

TINA BLACK

Who are the negative people in your life right now? How can you create magic for them?

BE A LEADER

Week 10

Love Those Who Have Hurt You

"Let it go. Who cares? Build a bridge and get over it."

— Winn Claybaugh

Last week I gave you the challenge to love negative people. How did you do? This week's challenge is to love those who have hurt you. I can guess what some of you are thinking: "What?!? Now Tina, you're going too far!"

Before you shut this book, keep reading. Listen, this message is directed just as much to me as it is to you!

Of course I've had my share of hurts ... by family, friends, my staff. I've been sued, robbed, and bullied. Twice as a salon owner, I've had a full staff walkout. I've had staff members quit without any notice, I've had a staff member "misplace" $80,000, and countless people have attacked my character, just to name a few.

A long time ago, I decided to live a lifestyle of forgiveness. I chose to love those who have hurt me, and I believe it has come back to me tenfold. And besides, who am I kidding? I've hurt people, too! I'm not perfect, and you're not perfect. I'm certain that on a daily basis we all make choices to ignore a family member; not listen to someone with 100 percent focus; and exhibit impatience, selfishness, or anger toward someone. We're going to hurt people. I don't know about you, but I am so grateful when a family member, friend, or staff member doesn't hold a grudge against me but instead extends me grace. In fact, if you are reading this and I have hurt you in the past, please forgive me. Better yet, let me know so I can sincerely apologize.

I do and will always continue to live a lifestyle of forgiveness. How about you? Will you? Trust me, it is a much, much easier existence with less anxiety, stress, frustration, and sickness.

This week, please take the time to think of someone or a list of someones who have hurt you. Extend forgiveness in your mind, verbally, or through a letter. Maybe you'll mail the letter to them, or maybe you'll throw it away— whichever you think will have the biggest impact on YOU. Yes, YOU! Trust me, your life will never be filled with more joy, less stress, and less anxiety. As my good friend and author Winn Claybaugh has taught me in his book *Be Nice (Or Else!)*, "Let it go, who cares, build a bridge and get over it!" (my mantra for years).

Thank you for loving those who have hurt you!

TINA BLACK

Think of someone (or a list of someones) who has hurt you. Extend forgiveness in your mind, verbally, or through a letter.

BE A LEADER

Week

Love Fear: It Will Make You Courageous

"Everything you want is on the other side of fear."

— Jack Canfield

Love fear. Long ago I heard statements such as "Do it afraid" or, as my good friend Sarah K. says, "Whatever you fear, do next." Now, I don't know about you but I only love fear and do what I fear sometimes. It's rare, but I've done it ... and when I've faced my fear, it feels darn good!

My speaking coach on the John Maxwell Team challenged me to turn in speaking videos to be critiqued on a weekly basis. At our training sessions, he would choose about 24 of us to present our messages. When my turn came, it was the first time I faced my fear of rejection and *I DID IT!* Standing in front of 1,000-plus people in that audience, I got a mad rush. The feeling of "I did it!" came over me as I sat down. I had faced my fear.

Okay, now that that's over .... on to the next fear. Oh my goodness, I have so many! Where do I start?!?!?!

Here's the challenge for me and for you. This week, write down all the things you fear and start on each one. One by one. Write down, "Whatever you fear, do next." Then develop a plan to get it done.

Love fear. It will make you courageous.

Come on, now! We've got this. We're in this together.

TINA BLACK

Do you love your boss?

Do you make your boss look good? How?

Do you love your coworkers? Do you make them look good?

What can you do more of? Less of? Stop doing? Start doing?

Week 14

Self-Pity: The Worst Form of Pride

"When you're good at something, you'll tell everyone. When you're great at something, they'll tell you."

— WALTER PAYTON

Have you ever experienced someone in your life who constantly reminds you how good he or she is, or someone who never lifts others up? How about you? How much time do you spend telling people how good you are ... or worse yet, how bad you are?

Too often, when something goes wrong in people's lives, I'll hear them say, "That's the story of my life," or "Nothing ever goes right in my life." That's the modern form of a pity party: consistently feeling bad for yourself. When I was 16, I went through that vice for about 2 years, always feeling sorry for myself. I was actually suicidal, and constantly wondering how I could stop the pain. It was a pity party gone wrong, until I found God and realized that my thoughts about myself were the sin of pride.

Feeling bad for yourself is the number-one form of pride you can have.

Pride = A peculiar kind of insanity caused by a lack of humility (www.seekfind.net)

I've learned through the years that lifting others up is a much happier countenance to have. Yes, I work on myself to grow, gain more confidence, and become an expert in various areas of my life but I spend less and less time feeling sorry for myself. Do I sometimes go through prideful, feeling-sorry-for-myself moments? Yep, I sure do ... such as 2 days after a major surgery I had in 2015 when I felt like no one cared and everyone was sick of helping me. Or one night when I fell in the bathroom, bruising my elbow and thigh (yep, I did ... you can stop laughing now!) and complained to my husband about how much pain I was in. But the next morning, after a rough night's sleep, I cleared my mind, feeling grateful to God for his mercies that I had not broken any bones.

My challenge to you this week is to listen to your thoughts and words about yourself. Check yourself. Do you have pride? Do you have pity parties? Do you feel sorry for yourself? A lot?

Spend some time lifting others this week. And remember: when you're good at something, you'll tell others but when you're great, they'll tell you.

TINA BLACK

How often do you have pity parties for yourself?

Listen to your thoughts and words about yourself this week and check yourself. How will you shift your thoughts? Your words?

Week 15

The Longer You Go Without Speaking, the Greater Weight Each Word Carries

"Just because you have a strong opinion doesn't mean you have to say it. The fashion in which you say it is more important."

— JUSTIN BLACK

Something my son Justin said a few years ago has really stayed with me.

I told him that the word I had chosen to focus on that year was *listen*. First, to listen to God during the day on what he'd have me do or say, and second, when in group meetings or staff meetings, to listen intently before I speak. My son said, "Just because you have a strong opinion doesn't mean you have to say it. The fashion in which you say it is more important."

He then reminded me of two stories in the Bible. The first one was about the woman who was caught in adultery. The religious leaders came to Jesus and asked, "What do you say, Jesus? The law says she is to be stoned to death." Jesus knelt down and, after a long silence, he wrote in the sand. Then he got up and said, "He without sin can cast the first stone." They all dropped their stones and walked away. It was the perfect answer at the perfect time. Jesus's words carried a lot of weight.

The second story took place when Jesus was on a boat. The disciples were freaking out because there was a storm but Jesus was down below, sleeping. At the right time, Jesus woke up and spoke just two words to the waves: "Be still!" Then he said to the disciples, "Why are you so afraid?" It was the perfect answer at the right time. Jesus's words carried a lot of weight.

There is power in our words but there is more power in listening. I'm challenging myself and challenging you to really listen in every opportunity you can. Whether it's with a client, friend, spouse, child, family member, coworker, or boss—really listen. Remember, as my son Justin says, "The longer you go without speaking, the greater weight each word carries."

This week, spend time listening. Be slow to answer and watch what happens.

TINA BLACK

On a scale of 1 to 10, with 1 being "not at all" and 10 being "all the time," how well do you listen? Now ask your family to grade you. How well do the scores match up?

What can you specifically do to be a better listener?

BE A LEADER

Week 16

Let Your Life Be a Prayer

"You have heard that it was said, 'Love your neighbor and hate your enemy.' But I tell you, love your enemies and pray for those who persecute you."

— MATTHEW 5:43–44

My husband and I made a pact a few years ago: every time we started to discuss someone in our lives (kids, family, staff, etc.) in a negative light or started to judge them, we would stop and pray for them together. This has honestly been the most transforming decision in my life, and I know my husband agrees.

This habit has helped me rid myself not only of controlling tendencies but also of anger, guilt, and frustration for the other person. It's given me new compassion for the person and a love for my enemies.

Go ahead and try it!

Here's the challenge:

Select someone or several people, if you have them in your life (your inner circle), and ask them to agree that every time one of you complains or mentions any negativity about another person that you will stop and pray together for that person instead. Remember, it takes at least one of you to be the leader in this. Make it a 21-day fast: fasting from negativity or gossip.

Do you need to fast from negativity or gossip? Who can be your accountability buddies in this?

BE A LEADER

Week
17

Keep the Momentum Going

"Momentum is a leader's best friend."

— JOHN C. MAXWELL

Every year I challenge my team to choose a word for the year instead of making a New Year's resolution. I've heard it said that three-fourths of resolutions are broken by January 15, but "one word" can change your life. I've proven this for the past few years. Choosing words such as love and patience has set me up for much-needed change in my life.

My daughter Brianna is so wise: in 2014, she chose the word *momentum* and she experienced one of her most momentum-building years ever. In one year she helped lead our education team to an overwhelming financial victory, was promoted to education director for all of our family's Paul Mitchell Schools, and became part-owner of a salon. That was a lot for a 23-year-old!

John Maxwell and many great leaders often say, "Momentum is a leader's best friend," and I ponder on that statement often. In 2015, my son's University of Northern Iowa football team lost their second playoff game. In the second half, they had started to build momentum and I could envision their potential win. Unfortunately, the offensive coordinator called a high-risk, trick play that failed. It stopped their momentum, threw the entire team off, and played a part in their defeat.

I thought, *Oh, I have another leadership message!* And here it is: if you know your team is building momentum, don't stop. Keep going.

I thought about all the times I've stopped momentum from happening to my team by making a frustrating call or not including them in my plans.

How about you? Have you ever experienced momentum in your life, only to sabotage yourself with laziness, indecisiveness, or a bad choice? Finish what you start. Stay positive. Stay focused. Don't quit. Do it afraid. Keep the momentum going. Momentum is a leader's best friend!

TINA BLACK

What one word did you choose for this year?

How can you build more momentum in your life right now?

What's one thing you need to complete today? This week? This month? This year?

How can you be sure to finish what you start? How will you build momentum? How will you keep it?

Week 18

No Worries, Mate!

"There's nothing to worry about, ever!"

— Scott Faye

Australians have a very popular saying: "No worries, mate!"

This makes me smile big time because I've spent most of my life worrying. Years ago, during a leadership mission project in Guatemala, I heard the best phrase ever by my mentor Scott Faye: "There's nothing to worry about, ever!" It became my number-one affirmation/mantra for over a year. I said it so often that even my staff took it on.

Whenever I started to worry, I would immediately say that mantra and feel my tense body relax. I actually visited my chiropractor and massage therapist less and less often; that simple affirmation saved me a lot of money!

Once in a while I slip back into my "worried stanza," but trust me, my family uses my own stuff on me.

How about you? Do you often worry or feel frustrated when something isn't going the way you envisioned? Do you have a dream that hasn't happened as quickly as you pictured it? I want to encourage you to press on and give the reins to God.

When I have a dream in my heart that doesn't seem to be happening, I play one of my favorite songs, *Press On*, by Selah. Some days I play it back to back, up to 10 times in a row, until I finally turn the control over to God.

Also, every day in my morning worship/journaling to God, I write the word *static* and list all my frustrations (sometimes my list is an entire page). When I'm done, I say, "God, I turn this all over to you." Immediately I feel calm and at peace, knowing that God has it all together for me and feeling thankful that I can begin to live that day the way God would want me to. Just like an Australian: "No worries, mate!"

TINA BLACK

Now you try it. What static or frustrations are you facing right now? Write them all down on a separate piece of paper. After you list them, write, "God, I turn this over to you." Then crumple the paper and throw it away.

How do you feel?

P.S. – I journal my static daily, and I love to look back weeks or months later to celebrate God's goodness in helping me.

BE A LEADER

Week 19

Hold Everyone Accountable

"In the best companies, everyone holds everyone else accountable—regardless of level or position."
— Yanky Fachler, The Bookbuzz Book of Biz Book Insights 2009

In their book *Crucial Conversations*, authors Patterson, Grenny, McMillan, and Switzler define a crucial conversation as a discussion where stakes are high, opinions vary, and emotions run strong. They say we can do three things when faced with crucial conversations: avoid them, face them and handle them poorly, or face them and handle them well. They add that the highest and most rewarded performers in business are those who face crucial conversations and handle them well.

How about you? Have you been routinely overlooked for a promotion at work? Do you wonder why the boss ignores you? Maybe it's because you aren't taking a risk and having that crucial conversation.

As a business owner, I need people on my team to step up to the plate. First of all, I'm human and I'm going to make mistakes, so if my staff members can hold me accountable, I know they will hold the slackers, gossipers, or dishonest team members accountable, too. And believe me, I have those people in my organization. We all do! But I only have two eyes, so I need my team to PLAY BIG and have crucial conversations all the time.

In the greatest companies, everyone holds each other accountable, regardless of their positions. I've heard statements such as, "I didn't want to throw them under the bus," or "I didn't want to be a tattletale." Come on now, who do you work for—your coworkers or the company? If you work for someone, be ALL IN. Be committed to the brand. Love what you do, who you do it with, and who you do it for. If you can't do that, then go get a NEW JOB!

For the past few years, I've been helping my key leaders in their personal and professional development, and we're getting so much stronger as a team. This has happened quite simply because of one thing: team members holding each other accountable. Not waiting for me, but taking it upon themselves to have crucial conversations with each other.

And here's one more benefit: Healthy communication can strengthen your immune system, help ward off disease, and increase your quality of life and well-being!

TINA BLACK

Do you avoid critical conversations with your coworkers? Your boss? Are you ALL IN at your current job? What shifts can you make today?

Who do you need to have a crucial conversation with? Now's your chance to practice your dialogue. Write it here ... then go do it!

BE A LEADER

Week 20

Don't Take Your Health for Granted

"Things you take for granted, someone else is praying for."

— Marlan Rico Lee

A few years ago, I attended the Children's Miracle Network Hospitals' Momentum event, which honors their Champions (kids who have received help financially), and what I saw blew my mind.

I saw children who were victims of bad health. I saw parents of children who'd been dealt a bad hand. I met amazing kids and amazing families.

I am blessed to be part of Paul Mitchell Schools, which have donated financially to Children's Miracle Network Hospitals for many years. I was equally blessed to witness this annual event and to meet all of the Champions chosen to represent their states in both the United States and Canada.

It made me realize how often I have taken my health for granted and how blessed I am to be healthy. As I've mentioned before, I had a cancer scare a few years ago that was quickly eradicated after major surgery. But some of these kids will not eradicate their diseases (including leukemia, mosaic trisomy, cystic fibrosis, diabetes, mitochondrial disease, Hutchinson-Gilford Progeria syndrome, myasthenia gravis, and heart defects, to name just a few).

I looked in their parents' eyes. Sometimes I saw fear. Sometimes exhaustion. Sometimes happiness. I especially connected with the moms. A mom's biggest fear is whether her kids will be born healthy or not. These kids were not. Praise God for Children's Miracle Network Hospitals, as they cover medical costs at upwards of $1 million a year per child.

I think about the times I don't eat healthy, don't sleep enough, don't exercise. Or better yet, the times that I hate exercising. Yet I *can* exercise (with few or no aches or pains as I age), while many of these kids will never exercise. Some of them may barely even walk.

How about you? Do you take your health for granted? Do you eat healthy? Exercise? Sleep enough hours at night?

Come on, now. Please don't take your health for granted. Do something. Do it now.

TINA BLACK

Do you take your health for granted?

Do you eat healthy? What shifts are you willing to make?

Do you exercise? What shifts will you make?

Get enough sleep? What lifestyle shifts can you make?

BE A LEADER

Week 21

React or Respond?

"Life is 10 percent what happens to me and 90 percent how I react to it."

— CHARLES SWINDOLL

One night, I heard late-night talk show host Jimmy Kimmel ask parents to participate in his annual "I told my kids I ate all their Halloween candy" YouTube challenge. He asked the parents to pretend they'd eaten all the candy, make a video of their kids' reactions, and post it on YouTube.

I thought it was pretty funny and pretty realistic, too. Some kids immediately reacted with tantrums, anger, and tears. Others had composure, forgiveness, and empathy.

It made me think about how I react as a leader when I receive bad news. Do I react or respond, and why? What causes me to react with anger, sadness, or immediate frustration? One thing I know for sure: when I haven't had enough sleep or I'm out of balance, I react. How about you? How do you react to alarming news?

TINA BLACK

How do you react to alarming news? What shifts can you make if your reaction is often negative? How will you do it?

BE A LEADER

Week
22

Get into the Game!

"Be all in or get all out. There is no halfway."

— UNKNOWN

After one of my son's football games at the University of Northern Iowa, he and I had an in-depth conversation about one of his teammates who really "gets into the games." Although this teammate didn't play a lot (for unknown reasons, because he is VERY talented!), he was always on the sidelines cheering on the players and really "getting into it," as my son said.

I said to my son, "Wow, this is another leadership message!" Could you imagine what might happen to our companies and our country if every follower and every employee just got into the game?

Instead, so many of us (and trust me, I did this when I was an employee) sit on the sidelines with our arms folded, thinking: *Why am I not playing? Why isn't the boss giving me attention? Why am I being ignored for this promotion? I'm clearly more talented than those people. My goodness, haven't you seen how many mistakes they keep making?*

As my son said, "You can never be too good for a job. Be all in. Put in the work for more, but don't be constantly focused on wishing for more. Be in the moment. Otherwise you put unneeded pressure on yourself. You'll be miserable until you achieve what you want, and then when you get it, you'll just want something more. But don't confuse being in the moment with being comfortable or complacent."

How about you? Do you want more but feel you're being overlooked in your current position? Are you in the game? Are you *really* in? Are you cheering on your teammates, your boss, and your clients? Are you happy for others who get promoted? Are you the biggest cheerleader in your business?

Take a good, hard look at yourself. Are you folding your arms and being complacent, or do you honestly know that you could do more, be more, and give more? Come on! GET INTO THE GAME!

TINA BLACK

Write down how you can "get into the game" more at your workplace.

How can you cheer on your teammates more?

How can you support your boss more?

Week 23

Set Up a Giving Plan, Not an Income Plan

"We make a living by what we get, but we make a life by what we give."

— Unknown

Paul Martinelli, president of the John Maxwell Team, was teaching a lesson called "The Seven Levels of Awareness." One of the levels is discipline, and Paul said the quickest way he became disciplined in all areas of his life began when he started to be obedient to God and tithe 10 percent.

I have pondered on that ever since and realized how right he was. That made me take it a step further and think about setting up a "giving plan" instead of an income plan.

Over the years, I've coached many staff members and students. It's amazing how many of them keep focusing on how much money they want to make but the discipline never happened to get them there.

I've heard it said that we release the same endorphins when we exercise as when we give back. This is so true! Being part of Paul Mitchell Schools, I'm on a high all day because our culture is all about creating magic, offering random acts of kindness, and giving back.

One time, I took my friend April to her chemo appointment (she had been getting chemo for almost a year, for breast cancer) and we handed out gift bags and love notes from my Future Professionals to some of the patients. I'll never forget the "high" I felt that day. I'm so grateful to April for that opportunity to give.

Can you imagine what might happen if you set aside time on your calendar to "create magic" and live a lifestyle of giving back? Our Paul Mitchell Schools have Be Nice Teams that do this. Why not form your own personal Be Nice Team and watch the endorphins flow? More happiness, more joy, and—who knows?—maybe even more money will just come to you. Go ahead! Set up a giving plan instead of an income plan and watch the blessings flow.

TINA BLACK

Take time to figure out how much money you want to tithe this year—to your religious organization, charities, etc.

Write down some ways you can give back this year (in time and money).

Week 24

Whatever You're Afraid of, Do Next!

"Do it afraid."
— SARAH KOBESKI

My husband and I celebrated our 28th anniversary in Hawaii, where our son had a football game against a Hawaii college team. We felt blessed beyond measure, to say the least.

It was our second trip to the Big Island and we decided to take in as much as we could. That required me to let my husband choose activities I would normally turn down. (Yikes!)

Two of those activities were a helicopter ride and then a small plane trip to view the Hawaiian Islands. Although the flights were breathtaking and the views were phenomenal, I would be less than honest if I didn't admit that I was deathly afraid of both trips.

Because I must practice what I preach, I couldn't say no, so I applied everything I have taught. Years ago, my dear friend and associate Sarah Kobeski taught me her mantra, "Do it afraid," which I repeated over and over in my head while going up in the air on both occasions. Trust me, a ton of Bible verses came to my head as well, and I said them over and over until they sank in and God gave me the perfect peace he always talks about... and, praise God, I'm alive to tell you my story! About halfway through (after I realized that I might not die), I started to calm down and enjoy the views. I kept thinking the entire time, "Oh boy, do I have another leadership message!"

Fear is in our faces on a daily basis, isn't it? If not, then we're not stretching ourselves to God's potential in our lives. As my dear friend Sarah taught me, whatever you fear, do next.

Here's another fear I overcame and something I'd wanted to accomplish for a long time: speaking to a group of businessmen and women. About 3 years ago, I was at a business meeting and thought, "Wow, I sure wish I could speak to this group some day." At the time it was only a wish, but 3 years later I did it: I taught a leadership class to them! My wish/dream was realized. No other feeling matches that sense of accomplishment. There's nothing better than adding value to people's lives and giving of yourself. Now on to my next fears!

Have you ever considered that the word *FEAR* stands for "False Evidence Appearing Real"? Fear is the one thing standing in our way of accomplishing our purpose. Don't let that happen to you. If this were to be your best year ever, what would you want to accomplish?

Now let's do this together. Let's DO IT AFRAID!

TINA BLACK

If this were to be your best year ever, what would you want to accomplish?

What are you afraid of accomplishing?

What do you long to do?

What dreams and goals have you always wanted to accomplish but never have?

What are you afraid of?

Go ahead, write them all down. Next to your list, write the words: DO NEXT!

Review the platform exercise from Week 12 and update your answers as needed:

1. On a scale of 1–10, how do you rate your life?

2. What would a 10 look like for you?

3. Why do you want your dream?

4. What are you willing to pay, do, or become to live your dream?

5. What are your current opportunities?

6. What are your strengths?

7. Who do you know that can help you?

8. What can you get rid of that no longer serves you?

In one sentence, who or what do you need to become so you can have what you want?

BE A LEADER

Week
25

When You Value Yourself, You'll Value Your Time

"Our days are like identical suitcases. Even though they are all the same size, some people are able to pack more into them than others. The reason? They know what to pack."

— Unknown

I had just packed my bag for a trip, and it brought to mind a story that John Maxwell shared in *Leadership Gold*. At a time-management seminar he attended, the presenter used this analogy to describe time: "Our days are like identical suitcases. Even though they are all the same size, some people are able to pack more into them than others. The reason? They know what to pack."

Successful leaders know when to delegate, when to say yes, and when to say no. They're focused. While most people fall into the "average" category, these brilliant leaders rise to the top because they know what to pack into a day, a week, and a year.

For my entire life, not managing my time has been one of my "excuses." When I first went into business, my husband would tell me to put things in my Google calendar. I'd laugh and say, "I don't need a calendar. I won't forget." And then, boom, I'd miss an important meeting and embarrassment would set in.

For years, I searched for some sort of system. My mentor Winn Claybaugh never forgot a meeting, a phone call, or an unanswered email. When I asked, "How do you do it?" he showed me his old-fashioned calendar. Then I learned that another mentor, fitness guru Chalene Johnson, puts everything on her Google calendar so I started doing that until, *bam*, I forgot my phone one day and missed an important meeting.

What was my problem? Focus. Believing in myself. When I started managing ME instead of trying to manage my time, things changed. Now I spend the first part of my day on my mental and physical health: I plan my day, then do a mental development activity (such as prayer, Bible study, or studying a leadership book), and then I work out. This routine dictates my day and my joy. On those days that I consider a "fail," I realize, "Tina, you didn't manage your time today!" For example, not long ago, I forgot an important appointment because I didn't use that first part of my day to plan.

How about you? What keeps you from valuing YOU? What limiting beliefs hold you back? Let go of those limiting beliefs and excuses and start becoming an expert in ME management. Remember, when you value yourself, you will value others, and you will value your time.

TINA BLACK

What time management system do you have in place? Is it working?

If not, what system can you adopt? And remember, it has to be fun, because if it's not fun, you won't do it.

How much time do you spend managing you? What system can you put in place now to do that? Can you take just 10 extra minutes a day? Can you get up 30 minutes earlier? What shifts are you willing to make?

Week 26

No More Excuses

*"If you're good at coming up with excuses,
you'll never be good at anything else."*

— UNKNOWN

I don't know about you but I often break promises to myself. I say I'm going to do something and then I cover it up with excuses. Those excuses often sound like, "Oh, I've been so busy" or "I've been traveling a lot," but when I get down to it, it's really fear holding me back. Fear of making mistakes. Fear of being transparent and showing my real self to others.

How about you? Have you made some promises to yourself? Maybe put some things on your calendar but never followed through with them? Have you said to yourself, "I'll get around to that someday"?

In the Mastermind groups I hold a few times a week, I always assign accountability partners in hopes that they will hold each other accountable to their promises. If you don't have an accountability partner, I encourage you to find one.

Come on ... Let's do this together. Let's make that someday now! Let's stop telling those lies to ourselves and to others around us. Listen to the words you say this week. I know I will.

TINA BLACK

What do you need to do that you've been putting off? Choose an accountability buddy to hold you accountable to it.

BE A LEADER

Week

Focus and Fun

"Focus and have fun."

— Alexis DeJoria

I remember when Alexis DeJoria, daughter of my business partner John Paul DeJoria, beat the world champion in the Funny Car division at the National Hot Rod Association (NHRA) U.S. Nationals, becoming the fourth female winner of the U.S. Nationals and the first woman to win three Funny Car races in a single season.

In an interview after the race, Alexis said something that moved me to tears, not only because a woman was making a mark in a traditionally male industry (of course) but also because of the way she thanked her team. Not once did she take full credit for her win, even though she was the only person in the car.

"It's a huge honor to represent such an incredible group of guys and a legend like [team owner and industry icon] Connie Kalitta, and I thank him every day for asking me to join their team," Alexis said. "It's really amazing to be the first woman to win three events in a year, but mostly I'm just so happy to have won this for Connie, Tommy [DeLago, crew chief], Glen [Huszar, co-crew chief] and my whole team, who has worked so incredibly hard, and it was great to get the job done today at such a huge race."

This is such a perfect example of being a level 5 leader (see John Maxwell's book *The 5 Levels of Leadership*). As Maxwell says, "None of us is better than all of us."

When the commentator asked Alexis how she did it, she said, "Focus and have fun." I loved this quote so much that I have been sharing it with the directors of my three schools—and I added "finish strong."

Focus, have fun, finish strong!

TINA BLACK

I often use this mantra as I finish out the year: "Focus, have fun, and finish strong!" How about you? What's your mantra for the rest of the year, personally, professionally, physically, emotionally, and spiritually?

BE A LEADER

Week

28

Lead with Love

"Whatever the question, the answer is love."

— Winn Claybaugh

This week I want to talk about the word *love*. I joined the John Maxwell Team in 2013. A few months later, 150 of us John Maxwell coaches went to Guatemala to train 25,000 leaders. Transformation in me began that week. Coincidentally, the word God had given me that year was *love*. A good work really began in me, something that my business partner and mentor Winn Claybaugh had taught me for years: "Whatever the question, the answer is love." That has always stuck with me, but I still have not graduated. I still fail at it every day, but I honestly feel like I've made great strides. I'm definitely not where I was.

How about you? Do you find yourself, like me, responding sometimes in anger or in rage to get what you want? Any time I get my way, such as by having temper tantrums or fits at my husband to get what I want, I lose. Any time we get our way by acting that way, we always lose. We have to die to selfishness to win. We have to lead with love.

I have been an entrepreneur for almost 20 years, and I can honestly say I did not always lead with love. In the past, the majority of my leading and accountability to my husband, kids, staff, etc., was with anger or fear. It took a while to sink in, but I finally realized that whatever the question is, the answer has to be love. Lead side by side. Honor the journey of the people next to me. Love them right where they are. Practice accountability with love.

I couldn't love others because I didn't love myself. I didn't feel worthy. My coach, Julie Gutierrez, challenged me to ask myself why I love God and why God loves me. And *bam*, there it was, looking me right in the face: was I worthy of God's love? Until recently I couldn't look myself in the eyes to say, "Tina, you are worthy. You are what God says you are." There are so many Bible scriptures to back up that message, and quite frankly, I memorized them until they sank deep inside of me. They have become my daily affirmations.

You see, you can't lead with love if you don't love yourself. My challenge to you is to fall back in love with yourself. Not the self-love filled with emptiness, shallowness, and selfishness that only leads to being miserable, but the God-love that allows you to surrender to him and know that he died for you, you are complete in him, and you can be who he says you can be.

TINA BLACK

Take time to answer these questions:

Why do you love God?

Why does God love you?

How can you fall back in love with yourself today?

Week 29

Leadership Begins and Ends with Integrity

"Like glue, trust bonds people together."

— Glenn Furuya

I read a great quote in a book given to me by Joannie Rossiter, my dear friend and owner of Paul Mitchell The School Hawaii. In *Little Book with 50 Big Ideas on Leadership*, author Glenn Furuya said, "Like glue, trust bonds people together." He then described the three "–rity" words that build trust:

- **Charity** – People will trust you when they believe that you are selfless. People trust hearts.
- **Clarity** – People trust leaders with clear visions. I am working on this; when explaining a business situation or challenge to my team, I keep saying to myself, "BE CLEAR, BE CLEAR, BE CLEAR!"
- **Integrity** – People trust leaders who walk their talk. Integrity is your character.

Everyone asks these questions of us as leaders: "Do you love me? Can you help me? Can I trust you?" When we demonstrate leadership in such a way that the answer to these questions is yes, we build connection. Connection always builds trust. We have to connect with people before we can ask for a hand, and no one has learned this more than me.

You see, being a "results-driven" leader made me skip over the connection part and become an "authority" type of leader. As John Maxwell has often said, 30 years ago authority was the way to lead; today, authenticity is the way to lead. People want to work *with* people, not *for* people. They want authentic leaders who are transparent, vulnerable, and have a more "human side."

How about you? Which kind of leader would you say you are? What kind of culture do you have in your business … at home … at church … in your organization? What do people say about you? If you don't know, ask them! Ask your clients, "Why do you shop here? Why do you do business with us?" Ask your kids what they think of you as a parent. Do you like what you hear? If not, what will you do to change it? What do you need to become? What no longer serves you?

TINA BLACK

Which kind of leader would you say you are? What kind of culture do you have in your business ... at home ... at church ... in your organization?

What do people say about you? If you don't know, ask them! Ask your clients, "Why do you shop here? Why do you do business with us?" Ask your kids what they think of you as a parent.

Do you like what you hear? If not, what will you do to change it? What do you need to become? What no longer serves you?

BE A LEADER

Week 30

With Crisis Comes Opportunity

"Sometimes you need a little crisis to get your adrenaline flowing and help you realize your potential."

— Jeannette Walls, The Glass Castle

For several years, Paul Mitchell Schools and John Paul Mitchell Systems have partnered to raise money and awareness for Bright Pink, a nonprofit organization that focuses on the prevention and early detection of breast and ovarian cancers in young women. A few years ago, I had the opportunity to participate with my school directors at Fabfest, a Bright Pink event in Cleveland, Ohio, where I spent time with Bright Pink founder Lindsay Avner. She blew me away with her courage, passion, and vision.

I now know more than ever why I had my personal crisis with cancer (with crisis comes opportunity): to help save lives from ovarian and breast cancer.

One in eight women will develop breast cancer in her lifetime. One in 67 women will develop ovarian cancer. Ovarian cancer is known as the "silent killer." Two-thirds of women diagnosed will die from this cancer.

But did you know ... When detected early, the survival rates are greater than 90 percent for both cancers?

I have never known a nonprofit for cancer that focuses solely on education and prevention, the way Bright Pink does. With knowledge comes power. With awareness comes action.

I know many of you, too, have suffered crises in your lives. In my book, *Be Amazing*, I shared many stories from people who have gone through adversity yet used it to their advantage. How can you use your crisis as an opportunity to strengthen you, your family, your community?

TINA BLACK

What crisis have you suffered?

How can you use this crisis to help others?

BE A LEADER

Week 31

Get Ready to Learn, Get Ready to Lead

"If you are not growing, you are dying."

— UNKNOWN

Every year, I host something called an "L2 leadership conference" in my Paul Mitchell Schools. Like all of the coaches for the John Maxwell Team, I've been given the opportunity to host these leadership simulcasts featuring valuable insights from John Maxwell and other bestselling authors and speakers. What a blessing it is to have local business owners in the room to experience these extraordinary events.

As a Paul Mitchell School owner since 2001, I have had the opportunity to not only train hairdressers but, through the leadership of Winn Claybaugh and John Paul DeJoria, the founders of Paul Mitchell Schools, to also change a lot of lives through the brilliant culture we teach. You see, we are one of the few educational companies in the world that recognizes that *talent is not enough to succeed in life: you must grow yourself personally to succeed, no matter what road you take.* We have always taught that personal development is 85 percent of your success; the rest is technical.

John Maxwell has a similar philosophy in his books and motivational teachings. Here are some of my takeaways from one of our previous L2 conferences:

1. Schedule a monthly meeting with people better than yourself and ask powerful questions such as: What's the greatest lesson you ever learned? What are you learning now? How has failure shaped your life? Who do you know that I should know? Will you help me meet them? What have you read that I should read? What have you done that I should do? How can I add value to you?

2. Stop being a helicopter parent, boss, and teacher. Put your hands in your pockets! Nothing propels success more than failure. Let the people around you fail. Don't micromanage.

3. Be as careful about what you put in your mind as what you put in your body. The first 45 minutes of the day are critical. Don't watch the news, read the news, or go online: media is negative programming. Start your day with gratitude and growth.

4. Don't just read a book: devour it.

5. Calendar your day and leave open spots. Give yourself time to think.

TINA BLACK

Which one of the takeaways from my L2 event can you use and apply right now? Write it down.

BE A LEADER

Week
32

Struggling Vines Produce Better Wines

"Don't quit. You're already hurting; you might as well get a reward for it."

— Eric Thomas

A few years ago, I visited Napa Valley. While touring one of my favorite vineyards, I spotted a great leadership message (of course!). The tour guide explained that California had been in a drought since 2011, but Napa had produced the best wines they've ever had during that time. When vines "struggle a bit," he said, they yield fewer grapes. Although the reasons aren't fully understood, those lower yields result in better grapes. In essence, the stressed ground produces better wines. The tour guide added that if the drought continued, it would harm the vines: they would need more rain by at least the following year to keep producing those brilliant crops and excellent wines.

That made me think about our lives. In people, just like in grapevines, a little stress can be beneficial but too much stress is bad. Balance seems to be the key.

Some of us seem so obsessed with being "in balance" that we forget we still need a little stress. Sometimes it seems that the people around me endure a little stress but then they give up. I'm on the outside looking in and thinking, "Come on, don't quit, you're closer than you think. Just don't quit!"

I get it, though. I've been in those shoes ... in fact, it happens to me all the time. I'll start a new project and run into so many roadblocks and resistance (even from my family) that I want to fold my cards and quit. Yes, even I want to quit sometimes. But something keeps nagging at me: "You're closer than you think, Tina. Don't quit!" And guess what? On those days when I'm ready to fold my cards, I'll get an encouraging text from someone in full support of the project, wanting to help me in any way they can. I know it must be God sending me a message not to quit!

How about you? Do you have one of those big hairy audacious goals (BHAGS), as my mentor Darren Hardy says, and you keep hitting resistance and feeling stressed, anxious, and frustrated?

I want to encourage you this week. Don't run from a little stress. Embrace it. Remember: struggling vines produce better wines.

And after all, isn't it more exciting to tell people about all the resistance and stress you went through to reach a goal?

TINA BLACK

Write down your BHAG (big hairy audacious goal) in this journal, and then write "I WON'T QUIT!"

Take out a separate piece of paper or sticky note and write "I WON'T QUIT" on that, too. Put it where you'll see it every day, such as your journal, planner, purse, or wallet. I like to keep mine on my computer desktop.

BE A LEADER

Week

33

Momentum: The Leader's Best Friend

"One way to keep momentum going is to have constantly greater goals."

— MICHAEL KORDA

A few years ago, I attended the Children's Miracle Network Hospitals' annual Momentum convention. Their president and advisory council reported that they had set a goal to start raising $1 billion a year by the year 2022. Until then, they'd been raising more than $300 million each year, and the amount had been steadily growing.

Children's Miracle Network Hospitals' primary fundraising efforts come from corporate fundraising campaigns with more than 80 corporate partners like Walmart, Sam's Club, Costco Wholesale, RE/MAX, Love's Travel Stops and Country Stores, and Paul Mitchell Schools. The funds flow directly to 170 affiliated children's hospitals throughout the United States and Canada.

This organization has built momentum every year, growing their funds by almost 50 percent for the 4 previous years. Their word for 2014 was *momentum* (thus the name of their event).

I heard that word a lot that year. First from my daughter Brianna, who chose it for her word. Her word proved true as our company in Fort Myers built momentum and grew our business over 20 percent.

In most of his books, John Maxwell says momentum is a leader's best friend. As he says, if we're not going forward, we're moving backward.

Think about how much easier it is to work out when you have momentum. If you're doing pushups or sit ups, for example, how much easier is it to go a little faster once you get started?

When you think of your life in all areas—professional, physical, emotional, spiritual—are you moving forward or staying the same (which is actually going backward)? How do you know? In what ways do you assess your life?

To assess the momentum in your life, fill out the balance wheel on the next page, and then set up an action plan to start building momentum.

If you're dragging your feet, do what my mentor John Maxwell teaches in *The 15 Invaluable Laws of Growth*: say "Do it now" 50 times.

Take some time right now to fill out the balance wheel on this page. Ask yourself: Am I growing in these areas? If not, why not? What do I need to stop doing? What do I need to start doing? What do I need to do more? Do less?

TINA'S BALANCE WHEEL

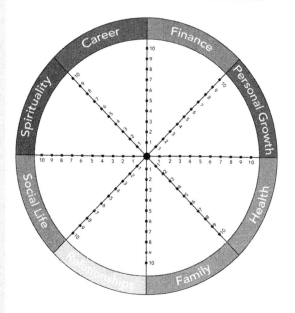

Take a few minuets to review the platform exercise from Week 12 and update your answers as needed:

1. On a scale of 1–10, how do you rate your life?

2. What would a 10 look like for you?

3. Why do you want your dream?

4. What are you willing to pay, do, or become to live your dream?

5. What are your current opportunities?

6. What are your strengths?

7. Who do you know that can help you?

8. What can you get rid of that no longer serves you?

In one sentence, who or what do you need to become so you can have what you want?

BE A LEADER

Week
34

5 Habits of Billionaire John Paul DeJoria
Habit #1: Use Technology Sparingly

"The human spirit must prevail over technology."

— ALBERT EINSTEIN

As a Paul Mitchell School owner, I am grateful to be business partners with John Paul DeJoria, cofounder of John Paul Mitchell Systems and majority owner of Patron Tequila. Recently, John Paul was featured on CNBC's *Follow the Leader* show, and he was amazing, to say the least. I can tell you firsthand that his personality and demeanor on the show were exactly the same as the man I know and love.

I loved the program so much that, for the next 5 weeks, I'm going to expand on John Paul's habits to encourage and challenge all of us to make them part of our habits as well.

If you missed it, you can watch the full episode of *Follow the Leader* at CNBC.com: http://cnb.cx/1RGETOR

John Paul's first habit is "Use Technology Sparingly." I honestly agree with this one, perhaps because, like John Paul, I'm not tech savvy, either, but mostly because I believe that a successful entrepreneur can't live behind a desk or a computer. To be a successful entrepreneur, you have to be with people. Every business is a people business, and we need to know how to connect with people so they'll buy what we're selling. And every business is selling something!

As John Paul recommends, leave technology to the experts. Hire people who can help you advertise. Social media is free, so be sure to use it. In my business it's how we keep in touch with our leads after we've connected in person. I have very few connections with whom I haven't connected to face-to-face first. Facebook, Twitter, and Instagram are my personal favorites and social media has become a bit of a second job for me; however, I hire people to keep it current in all of my businesses.

I do get a lot of emails, and my rule of thumb has always been to answer them within 24 hours; however, I often get behind so I'm working on several systems to keep them current.

TINA BLACK

How do you keep from getting inundated or carried away with social media and email? What percentage of your day is spent with people? Making connections? Inspiring them to do their jobs? Inspecting their performance? Connecting with your team to show them you care about them as people?

What can you do more of?

What can you do less of?

BE A LEADER

Week
35

5 Habits of Billionaire John Paul DeJoria
Habit #2: **Waste No Time on Wardrobe**

"Classy is when a woman has everything to flaunt, but chooses not to show it."

— UNKNOWN

I agree 100 percent with this one. You'll probably be surprised to hear that I dislike shopping. It's true. I'd rather work than shop. I find it frustrating, and trying on clothes feels like a workout ... and not the fun kind! Shopping feels like such a time-waster: I could be working on my craft or my business but instead I'm looking for outfits.

To John Paul's message, I would also add: why waste time and money on cheaper clothes? You'll actually save time by buying a few more expensive outfits and wearing them longer. I've personally wasted (and sometimes still do) so much money on cheap clothes, only to wear them a few times.

In our company we are required to wear black (we can accessorize with color). I can honestly say that the all-black look is both easy and timeless. Even if you prefer colorful clothes, look for easier ways to buy them, such as shopping online. Choose a few favorite stores instead of wasting days going through 50 of them. Personally, I love the White House Black Market store, where I can go into the fitting room and staff members bring me clothes they think I'd like to try on. I can do all of my shopping in a few high-quality hours and get on with my day. I've even heard of shop-online programs where you can rent an outfit for a month and buy it or ship it back. Now, that's something I need to look into trying!

Some of you are probably thinking, *But Tina, shopping is a bit of a sport for me and I love it.* And I'm thinking, *Really? You can't find other sports?* How about working out? Or going to the gym? Or reading a good leadership book to help your business?

John Paul is successful for a reason. We should listen to him. The bottom line is, stop wasting time! Now, before you reply with hate mail, how about at least narrowing down your shopping to two or three stores, or one or two online shopping venues? Your paycheck and your family are counting on you to use your time wisely.

TINA BLACK

How about you? Are you a shop-aholic? How will you make a shift in this area?

BE A LEADER

Week
36

5 Habits of Billionaire John Paul DeJoria
Habit #3: **Lean on Your Kids for Advice**

"You learn as much from your kids as they learn from you."
— TOM WAITS

Are you loving John Paul DeJoria's advice so far on five of his successful habits? Are they shocking you? Honestly, the more I dig into them, the more I realize how practical they are and how true they are in my life as well.

The first two were use technology sparingly, and don't waste time on wardrobe. Ready for the third habit? Lean on your kids for advice.

"Well," you might be saying, "my kids are too young," or "I don't have any kids." Then I say lean on those who know you best. The ones who truly have your back, not the ones who tell you what you want to hear. I loved it on the show when John Paul said he often goes to his daughter Alexis for advice because she has no problem speaking up. John Paul said he's surrounded with so many yes people and he knows his daughter will give it to him straight.

I was so glad he said that because that's exactly what I've done with my kids since they were born, especially with my daughter Brianna. She's been around my business since she was 6 years old and she's never missed a beat. Sitting in on dinner meetings or conversations I had with her dad, she'd sometimes speak up and say something profound. In those moments, I knew she'd be my eventual replacement. I always tell people she's a new and improved version of me, and it's true. She has all the positive characteristics of her dad and many of mine as well. She's also my hair and wardrobe stylist. I rarely wear an outfit or hairstyle that isn't approved by her first!

Brianna and I are now business partners in a salon venture. To be honest, she's been running the salon virtually on her own with very little input from her father and me.

I often lean on Brianna for personal and business advice. The same is true with my son Justin. He's very intuitive with people and he just gets it. So often I'll run things by him. He gives me sound business advice and out-of-the-box ideas that expand my mind.

Try it on! As John Paul says, when you need input, rely on those closest to you.

TINA BLACK

Who in your family can you get business advice from? Who tells you when you suck? Who encourages you the most in your dreams and pushes you beyond your comfort zone?

BE A LEADER

Week

37

5 Habits of Billionaire John Paul DeJoria
Habit #4: **Splurge for Convenience**

"Time is money."

— BENJAMIN FRANKLIN

Are you ready for John Paul's fourth habit?

We've already talked about using technology sparingly, wasting no time on wardrobe, and leaning on your kids for advice. Now here's number four: Splurge for convenience.

I agree 100 percent with this one! Now, obviously I don't have a private jet or a personal chef, but I can tell you in my own little way and with a much smaller bank account (compared to John Paul's), I have never cut back on convenience. Mind you, when my husband and I were first married we could only afford the salad bar for dinner at a local grocery store, but we ate healthy and were right there in the store, so we could eat and shop at the same time. Funny thing, we have a great grocery here in Michigan and we still do the same thing ... eat at their mini restaurant while we grocery shop. It's not only convenient; it's also fast and fun.

In everything I do, I know I have to spend money to make money. From the minute I started working, I've always hired someone to clean my house because I knew that doing it myself took time away from my job and meant less money for me. I've always splurged on slightly more expensive clothes because they wash better (don't have to waste time ironing) and last longer. In everything I do, I ask myself, "Is it necessary? Is it convenient?" If the answer is no, then I rarely do it.

TINA BLACK

Look around you. Where can you splurge for convenience? Make a bucket list and set a budget on where you can splurge. Time is money—don't forget that!

Week 38

5 Habits of Billionaire John Paul DeJoria
Habit #5: Stay Positive

"Stay positive, even when it feels like your whole world is falling apart."

— UNKNOWN

I will admit, I'm probably one of the most positive people I know. However, unlike John Paul DeJoria (and my husband, I might add), my positivity scale plummets under pressure, adversity, or pain. I tend to freak out ... a lot. And complain ... a lot. Thank God for my husband because he calms me. I also repeat this affirmation over and over to calm myself: "There's nothing to worry about ever."

How about you? Are you positive? Especially when bad things happen? Or do you whine, moan, and complain? The first step is awareness. If you're not sure, ask those closest to you. Then, if you're like me, set an accountability plan for those moments because I honestly believe the universe won't grant you more to take care of until you can take care of what you already have (properly, and with a positive attitude).

One of my accountability plans is a daily gratitude journal. The first thing I do when I wake up is journal what I'm grateful for from the day before. Then I write down all my "static" (that's a nice word for challenges), and after I write it out I give it all over to God and repeat my mantra: "There's nothing to worry about, ever." Then I spend time meditating on God's word and praying. Then I work out at the gym or with one of my Beachbody at-home workouts. These are my default habits to keep me positive. Without them ... well, you don't want to know what happens to me!

Now, go get positive and change the world!

Again, in case you missed it, here's the link to Follow the Leader featuring John Paul DeJoria: http://cnb.cx/1RGETOR

TINA BLACK

Practice journaling.

What are you grateful for?

What challenges are you currently facing?

There's nothing to worry about ever! God has this!

BE A LEADER

Week 39

Game On!

"You can't make up for a lack of reps."

— Unknown Sports Announcer

During football playoff time, the TVs in our home have football games going nonstop. One day, while half listening / half dozing, I heard an announcer talking about a quarterback and saying, "You can't make up for a lack of reps." In my sleepy slumber state, I grabbed my notepad to write down the leadership message I heard in that statement!

Although I'd had over 18 years in the salon business, owned several schools, and had gotten back into the salon business a few years earlier in a partnership with my daughter, I still didn't consider myself an expert in the field.

I've heard it said that it takes 10,000 hours of experience to become an expert, but I think the experts really mean *evaluated* experience. I think of all my "lousy" years as an owner/leader when I thought I was better than I was. I wasted a lot of time not evaluating my effectiveness or evaluating and learning from my mistakes. I think of all the time I could have avoided wasting if I had just hired a salon coach.

I'm finally waking out of my sleepy slumber of reality. Thank you, John Maxwell Team, for opening my eyes to my reality and what it would take for me to become an expert.

You can't make up for a lack of reps. If you want to improve, you must play the game. Win or lose. Learn. Keep grinding. Keep growing. Game on!

What do you want to be an expert in? What are you striving to do, become, or specialize in? What are you willing to do to get more reps? Are you willing to risk everything to do it?

My challenge for you this week is to grab your journal and spend 30 minutes writing down what you want to be an expert at. Then write down what you need to do more of, less of, stop doing, and start doing this year to get there. Game on!

TINA BLACK

What do you want to be an expert at?

Are you willing to risk everything to do it?

What are you willing to sacrifice to make it happen?

What will you do more of? Less of? Stop doing? Start doing?

BE A LEADER

Week

Leadership Lessons I Observed in Africa

"Great leaders do not desire to lead but lead to serve."

— MYLES MUNROE

Since 2007, Paul Mitchell Schools have donated $830,000 to help Food 4 Africa feed 10,000 orphans each day. In May 2016, my husband and I got to see firsthand how the money is used when we traveled with a team from the nonprofit Coco's Foundation (www.cocosfoundation.co.uk), which partners with the nonprofit Food 4 Africa (www.food4africa.org) to feed, clothe, and build shelter for families in South Africa.

I've been on many mission trips before (Mexico, Haiti, Guatemala) so seeing the poverty was not a shock; however, this trip had a whole new meaning for me.

During those 2 weeks, I observed 10 leadership lessons that I'd love to share with you.

Lesson #1: Be a Servant Leader

For the past 6 years, Chris Connors, founder of Coco's Foundation, has organized teams three to four times a year to build homes and make a difference in the area he serves. Chris could just collect money to feed the Africans and build homes, but instead he gives volunteers the chance to immerse themselves in the community and get to know the people they are serving. He takes people on this mission trip to change their lives and he offers an opportunity like no other nonprofit I know.

I have never seen a servant leader like Chris before: he is one of the most selfless human beings I've ever met and he has a heart for people you don't often see. I observed him during the entire 2 weeks, and not once did he waver from his servant leadership. He represented what I strive to be.

This made me wonder: How much of a servant leader am I? How can I become a better servant leader? How can I help my team become better servant leaders?

TINA BLACK

My questions to myself and to you this week are:

Do I have a servant's attitude when it comes to leadership?

In situations where I am required to serve others, how do I respond? Am I impatient? Am I resentful? Do I believe that certain tasks are beneath me or my position in the company?

How can I better serve my team this week?

Week 41

Leadership Lessons I Observed in Africa
Lesson #2: Build Solid Relationships First

"People don't care how much you know until they know how much you care."
— JOHN C. MAXWELL

Before you try to help people, sell them something, or coach them to greatness, the ONLY way to successfully earn their trust is to build a solid, appropriate relationship. I first earned this from John Maxwell's book, *The 5 Levels of Leadership*. Anyone can be appointed to a position, but people only follow you because they want to—and usually only because they like you.

I used to try to get my team to produce results without first getting to know them and what they desire. I treated my people as if they were a paycheck. I'd often hear myself asking, "Why can't they just do their job? I give them a paycheck, don't I?" After reading and studying John Maxwell's book, I realized I'd had it all wrong. I've mentioned many times that I was mostly a great employee for every job I worked in before I became a business owner—but now that I look back on it, I realize it was because my bosses always took time to get to know ME. They genuinely cared about me. My last employer and his wife were perfect examples of that. They always pulled me aside to get to know me. Always asked questions about my husband, my family, my life. They were people-people! No wonder their team never leaves them. No wonder they are so successful.

In Africa, I observed Chris Connors with the people whose homes we were building and the people he hired to build those homes. Even though most of them don't speak English, Chris has managed to find people in Africa who trust him and visa versa. He did this through mostly nonverbal language: hugs, giving of gifts that they actually need or want, and smiles. Chris genuinely cares, and you can tell that the people FEEL it. Just like John Maxwell says, "People don't care how much you know until they know how much you care." You can't speak into people's lives if they know you don't genuinely care about them.

How about you? Are you the kind of leader who says, "Why can't they just do their job? They get a paycheck"? I want to challenge you to read *The 5 Levels of Leadership* and work to gain influence by building solid relationships with your team.

Even if you don't have the title of "leader" on your team, the quickest way to gain influence is by building solid relationships with everyone you work with. And if you need to coach or redirect people, they won't listen unless they know you genuinely care about them. Building solid relationships makes life at work so much easier. Trust me. Now go do it!

TINA BLACK

Ask yourself these questions from **The 5 Levels of Leadership:**

Do I know things about every person on my team's family and personal life outside of work?

Do I know every person on my team's strengths and weaknesses?

Do I know every person on my team's hopes and dreams?

Am I committed to helping every person on my team succeed in his/her work?

Does every person on my team trust me, and do I trust them?

BE A LEADER

Week 42

Leadership Lessons I Observed in Africa
Lesson #3: One Is Too Small a Number to Achieve Greatness

"No accomplishment of real value has ever been achieved by a human being working alone."

— JOHN C. MAXWELL, LEADERSHIP GOLD

This quote comes from John Maxwell, and it is SO TRUE! I'm in the hair industry and I'm always perplexed by the number of hairstylists who would rather rent a chair and work alone than have a team to support and cheer them on. I guess they choose to do it not because they will make more money (most do not) but because they don't like their boss or their coworkers. That makes me want to step up my game as a leader and make sure I communicate often with my team and recognize when they are disenchanted with my leaders or me.

In his book, *The 21 Irrefutable Laws of Leadership,* John Maxwell often talks about the Law of Influence. He says, "If you don't have influence, you'll never be able to lead others." I observed this leadership quality in Chris Connors in Africa. He had a dream to help people but he knew he was only one person. To develop the area and serve the Africans, he would need to influence others around him. He knew that "one is too small a number to achieve greatness," so he reached out to Winn Claybaugh, dean and cofounder of Paul Mitchell Schools, to see if a few students could come out to help build homes. Chris knew that if he could "influence" them he would have more people who would believe in his cause.

As you know, instead of two students he got two school owners: my husband and me. We fell in love with the South African people and now we want to help them as well. Like Chris, we need to influence those around us to join our cause, because one is too small a number to achieve greatness.

While talking about the Law of Influence in *The 21 Irrefutable Laws of Leadership,* John Maxwell says the only way to persuade people to follow you is to become a better leader. To become a better leader, you have to strengthen 7 core qualities (character, relationships, knowledge, intuition, experience, past success, and ability) and become the kind of leader others want to follow.

TINA BLACK

Here's a way to stretch your influence that John Maxwell talks about in his book:

This week, try to influence someone you never have before—a supervisor, a colleague, a follower in your sphere of influence, or a family member or close friend. Test your influence. Write about how you do: your successes, your struggles, and your plan to gain more influence over those around you.

Week 43

Leadership Lessons I Observed in Africa
Lesson #4: Leaders Must Give Up to Go Up

"For everything you have missed, you have gained something else; and for everything you gain, you lose something else."

— RALPH WALDO EMERSON

Talk to any leaders who have done something significant and they will tell you they have made trade-offs. In Africa, I repeatedly saw this in Chris Connors. I can only imagine the worry, the fear, and the late nights he spends trying to figure out how to pay for the next home and the next meal. He has given up so much to make this all happen.

I also saw it in Rachel and Victor, who gave up their lives in England and transported their family to serve the people of South Africa. Barely a day goes by when they don't have someone staying in their home or joining them for a meal. Every evening while we were there, Rachel made dinner for all 10 of us plus some of the locals. And they weren't ordinary dinners—they were made from scratch and typically took from two hours to the majority of the day to prepare.

It's perplexing for me to imagine that Rachel doesn't make dinner for just herself and her husband. Or have date nights with him. Or time alone. It's hard for me to imagine that they don't see their married children as often as some families do. Rachel was taking care of an orphanage that burned down some months ago, and I can't imagine her worries for the displaced orphans with nowhere to go. Victor is a doctor in the community and I can only imagine his daily worry as he tries to save lives. What they have given up is astounding to me.

The needs are so great in South Africa, and I have been trying to put together a team and get them excited to go there and help. I feel overwhelmed with grief and sick with worry that it won't happen. Some nights I can't sleep because I'm worried I won't influence enough people to want to make a difference. I'm only trying to give up a few weeks of my year—I can only imagine the frustration and worry that Chris, Rachel, and Victor have. What they've given up I would never give up. John Maxwell calls it the Law of Sacrifice: you have to give up to go up.

Do you have a dream so big you can taste it? The truth is, you have to sacrifice some things for your dream to happen—time, ego, money, just to name a few. But there may be other things you are unwilling to sacrifice.

TINA BLACK

Here's your challenge for this week...

Make two lists:

Write down the things you are willing to give up to go up.

Write down the things you are unwilling to sacrifice in order to advance.

For example, I'm willing to give up money and risk it all to make things happen in my life. I am willing to give up time, and I am willing to give up my fear of failure. But I am unwilling to give up my health and my marriage to advance.

Now write a statement:

For 6 months I will give up _____
_____

And instead I will _____
_____

*My goal is to*_____

I will tell _____
about my progress and ask this person to hold me accountable.

(Adapted from **21 Laws of Irrefutable Leadership***)*

Week

Leadership Lessons I Observed in Africa
Lesson #5: Leaders Know They Are Only As Strong As Their Weakest Link

"A chain is no stronger than its weakest link, and life is, after all, a chain."

— WILLIAM JAMES

When we were in Africa, the second of the two homes we built went a lot slower because two of the missionaries got sick. I didn't feel so hot that week, either. I'm guessing we all ate something that made us all feel ill, which is common when traveling abroad. The heat was exhausting, too, and I noticed that I didn't work as hard on the second house as I normally would. In fact, the whole team worked with less enthusiasm than the week before. We only completed three-fourths of the house before we left, but I bet if we had all been feeling 100 percent well, we could have built the whole house.

It is so true that when one team member is down, the whole team falls because of it. We're only as strong as our weakest link. I've witnessed that too often in my businesses, and I'm sad to say I've barely addressed it through the years. I've been much more aware of it these past few years, and together with my company's leaders, we're addressing it more and more. It's not an area we can overlook in our businesses.

This realization has also made me ask myself if I'm the weakest link in my family, the community organizations I belong to, my church, etc. I honestly feel like I often am and I now know that I need to either quit that organization or get on board 100 percent.

How about you? In your business, job, organization, which one are you—the strongest or the weakest link? Your business, organization, or team will never hit their goals or achieve their dreams until everyone gets on board.

TINA BLACK

Take some time to evaluate this week:

- In my business or organization, are we hitting our goals?
- In what ways do I prove I'm not the weakest link in my business?
- In what ways can I improve myself to be a better team player and be the strongest link?

Week 45

Leadership Lessons I Observed in Africa
Lesson #6: Leaders Read Between the Lines

*"Great leaders find ways to connect with their people
and help them fulfill their potential."*

– STEVEN J. STOWELL

Successful leaders apply what John Maxwell calls the Law of Intuition: they can always sense their people's hopes, fears, and concerns. They always know when their team members are at 100 percent, and if anyone slips below, they address it immediately.

I witnessed that with Chris Connors in Africa. Every day, he checked in with every one of us missionaries. If we were struggling, he knew it, he addressed it, he helped us find solutions, and we'd move on. There was never a time when we didn't feel cared about or supported.

Chris knew this about the South Africans, too. He visits the same people four to five times a year so he always knows if something is "up" with one of them, even though they barely speak English. I often witnessed him hugging people and taking time to listen to them.

Watching Chris made me ask myself, *Am I that way with my team?* I definitely have some work to do when it comes to the Law of Intuition. I need to get better at reading between the lines.

How about you? How do you do with your team? Your family? Your friends? Do you, too, have some work to do in this area?

Three ways to improve your intuition are to read books on relationships, learn how to ask better questions of people, and study their nonverbal communications. (Be a people watcher!)

Some great books by John Maxwell include:

Everyone Communicates, Few Connect

How to Influence People

Good Leaders Ask Great Questions

I also recommend Stephen Covey's book, *7 Habits of Highly Effective People*.

TINA BLACK

Take time this week to evaluate your skills in reading between the lines.

- *What can you do more of?*
- *What can you do less of?*

Week 46

Leadership Lessons I Observed in Africa
Lesson #7: Leaders Make Growth Their Responsibility

"Before you are a leader, success is all about growing yourself. When you become a leader, success is all about growing others."

– JACK WELCH

After becoming a John Maxwell coach, I learned what separates great leaders from good leaders: great leaders invest in those who follow them. Just as leaders need their own growth plans, we also need to set up growth plans for those who work for us. One thing I love about being a Paul Mitchell School owner is that we provide additional education for our teams and a solid career path so they can grow technically. As a John Maxwell coach, I have also set up a system to help my team grow emotionally, because emotional intelligence trumps IQ.

Show me a staff member who excels in being aware of his or her own strengths and weaknesses and has a plan to develop them, and I will show you a successful staff member for life. Too often, staff members fail in their positions or they lack results or performance because they lack emotional intelligence: they lack in areas such as assertiveness, stress tolerance, change tolerance, anger management, social skills, accountability, flexibility, empathy, decision making skills, and communication skills, just to name a few.

In South Africa, I observed that Food 4 Africa and Coco's Foundation not only provide food and homes for the families, but they also provide emotional intelligence training and afterschool classes for the students. Most of these children are orphans whose grandparents, siblings, or extended families take care of them. These kids have very little access to life training, and it makes me proud to support organizations that provide this important training and focus on the growth of the people they serve. The main goal behind the classes and training is to provide emotional support and strategies to help people overcome their losses.

One thing I am working on in all of my businesses is a *solid plan* for emotional intelligence training, including professional and emotional development for every member of our teams. I want to make growth my responsibility so no team members ever want to leave our company again.

TINA BLACK

How about you? Do you work for a company? Does your company have a solid plan for growth? Remember, leaders make growth their responsibility!

What is your growth plan this year?

Week 47

Leadership Lessons I Observed in Africa
Lesson #8: Who You Are Is Who You Attract

"Become better and you attract better."

— UNKNOWN

John Maxwell calls this the Law of Magnetism; he says teams are seldom determined by what we want, but more by who we are. This discovery was truly a game changer for me. After losing and having to fire so many staff members during my years as an entrepreneur, I suddenly learned that to get eagles working for me I had to stop being a duck and become an eagle.

Trust me, I still have a long way to go but I can tell you this: I *WILL NOT* stop growing. Why? Because I'm beginning to really know my strengths and I definitely know my weaknesses. Every day I look in the mirror and ask myself, "Okay, Tina, who can you hire to cover your weaknesses?" I look at my leaders each day, and think, "Tina, how can you support your leaders to hire and staff their weaknesses?" And better yet, "What growth plan can I put my leaders on so they feel empowered to put their teams on a growth plan? How can I get my leaders to never settle for mediocrity (ducks) on the team and raise up eagles? How can I inspire them?"

Real leadership is about helping my team transform themselves, and the only way I can do that is to transform myself. When they see me grow and become better, they desire to invest in growth themselves. When I see my leaders investing in their own growth—picking up a book or listening to a podcast without my nudging and telling me about it, investing in their own growth seminars—I know I have empowered successfully. You see, it's not just about our team doing their jobs; it's about our team investing in themselves personally and professionally. Leadership truly starts at home, and if I can help them see that, everything changes in their lives and our business.

I witnessed the Law of Magnetism in Chris Connors and the team he chose to join him on our mission trip. Every one of us was like-minded and had a desire to serve. Every one of us had a desire to grow. Every night Chris videotaped what we learned that day, and there was not one day that one of us failed to grow from the experience there. How much better could we all be if we videotaped ourselves at the end of the day—every day of our lives—and said, "This is what I learned today"?

Chris Connors truly is a brilliant leader and I am so glad I met him and learned to stretch my mind to think differently. How about you—do you have a Chris in your life to make you stretch and think differently? Someone who won't settle for your duck status and will instead push you to want to become an eagle?

TINA BLACK

I have two challenges for you:

1. Find a mentor to stretch you and start stalking him or her. (P.S., that's my first step to success in my book, **Be Amazing**). If you haven't picked it up yet, you can order it at http://emerge-books.myshopify.com/products/be-amazing

2. My second challenge is to daily or weekly record a video of yourself telling what you learned, how you were stretched, and how you grew personally and professionally that week.

BE A LEADER

Week 48

Leadership Lessons I Observed in Africa
Lesson #9: Get Comfortable Being Uncomfortable

*"Get comfortable being uncomfortable.
That's how you break the plateau and reach the next level."*

— CHALENE JOHNSON

My trip to Africa was no ordinary mission trip. I like to call it a mission trip with a twist! For example, after we built our first home in South Africa, our leader Chris Connors surprised us with a trip to an African safari. "After all," he said, "what's a trip to South Africa without going to a safari?"

As we drove up to the safari we saw zebras and monkeys randomly running near the sides of the road. It was a sight to see. Chris, knowing how much I love zebras, stopped several times so I could take pictures. When we got to the safari, it was like nothing I'd ever seen before: animals roaming around in their natural habitats, including many animals I'd never heard of before. Giraffes everywhere. I felt like I was in the movie *Jurassic Park*.

On our jeep tour we were blessed to see lions off in the distance. (Thank goodness they sleep during the day.) A zoo pales in comparison and a safari is a must, so be sure to put it on your bucket list.

On the last day, Chris had another surprise for us: to touch and pet elephants. I'm not going to lie: that has never been on my bucket list. And honestly, it was raining and cold and I wanted to say, "No, go ahead. I'm good." But then I remembered this leadership principle: get comfortable being uncomfortable.

Trust me, I was definitely not comfortable with the idea of standing under an elephant that could crush me at any moment if he desired. And to top it off—to have to touch his tongue? Oh my! It would take a few days to wash that off! But I can honestly tell you that when I finished I felt a huge sense of achievement. I felt so proud of myself that I could tackle anything.

Maybe you're thinking, *Tina, I'd love to do that. Why were you so scared?*

Well, you might have something you need to get comfortable with, too. Maybe it's speaking in front of your peers. Maybe it's talking to your boss. Maybe it's reaching out to a mentor you're intimidated by. Maybe it's joining a gym to get healthier. Maybe it's writing a book. Maybe it's starting your own business. Whatever it is, all you need is 20 seconds of insane courage. Count to 20 and just do it!

TINA BLACK

What's on your bucket list that you've been putting off and can't put off anymore? What's that one thing you need to do to catapult you to the next level at work or in your business? Write it down, then count to 20 and do it.

Get comfortable being uncomfortable!

BE A LEADER

Week

Leadership Lessons I Observed in Africa
Lesson #10: Get Your Leadership On!

"The problem with most people is that you're not obsessed with improvement."

– Eric Thomas

My daughter Brianna and I love to teach a class for salon and school owners called "Get Your Leadership On!" Most classes teach you how to succeed in business, but few teach you how *not* to fail or the biggest reasons for failure. That's why we put this class together, and let me tell you, salon and school owners love it because it includes all the things they wish they could say but never actually say. After the class, most of them thank us and tell us they now have the courage to have those crucial conversations with their staff members.

Many people fail in business because they lack the self-awareness and self-management skills required for success. In other words, they can't manage their emotions. I've been studying emotional intelligence quite heavily, and one thing is for sure: in most cases, emotional intelligence trumps IQ.

When I was in Africa I noticed that Chris Connors constantly recognized the emotional ups and downs of our teams. He knew when team members were struggling to get along and when they were struggling emotionally, especially after witnessing the devastation in the areas we served. I'm not going to lie: it never gets easier to see people struggling for their very existence. I wanted to pack all of the children into my suitcase and bring them all home, but that wouldn't solve anything. We need to teach people how to give a hand up, not a handout—and Chris is a genius at this. He knew exactly how to turn a situation around and how to get our team to laugh. He knew how to connect one-on-one and always made time to do it. I may never be as skillful as Chris at this, but I want to be better because I know it will take my businesses to the next level.

I know I need to constantly get my leadership on, and the way to do it is to always have a growth plan. It's easy for me now because I belong to the greatest leadership company in the world, the John Maxwell Team, and through their mentoring program I have access to a plethora of courses I can take and teach to my teams.

How about you? Do you have a growth plan? Do you know your strengths and weaknesses? Do you have a plan to develop them? How can you get your leadership on?

Take time to write out a growth plan for the rest of the month, the next quarter, and the next year. Then get your leadership on!

Before we wrap up the 10 leadership lessons, let's recap them one more time.

Leadership Lessons I Observed in Africa:

1. *Be a Servant Leader*
2. *Build Solid Relationships First*
3. *One Is Too Small a Number to Achieve Greatness*
4. *Leaders Must Give Up to Go Up*
5. *Leaders Know They Are Only as Strong as Their Weakest Link*
6. *Leaders Read Between the Lines*
7. *Leaders Make Growth Their Responsibility*
8. *Who You Are Is Who You Attract*
9. *Get Comfortable Being Uncomfortable*
10. *Get Your Leadership On!*

Week

Do You Have the Heart of a Finisher?

"When you are tempted to give up, your breakthrough is probably just around the corner."

— JOYCE MEYER

I heard a great message from Christian author and speaker Joyce Meyer about putting your dreams to the test and finishing what you start. It's easy to start something. In fact, people all over the world start New Year's resolutions, but by January 15 about 95 percent of them have already stopped.

What were your goals for this year? Did you complete them? As I look back at the goals I set for myself this year, I feel great about them.

Each year, I usually have some small tweaks to finish out my goals, so I add them onto next year's list and set a plan to complete them.

How about you? What three goals do you want to complete before the end of this year, to have your best year ever?

Maybe you want to get out of debt, or make your marriage stronger, or get healthy again, or get organized. Or maybe you just want to get back on track with setting goals.

Remember to finish what you start. My challenge for you is to have the heart of a finisher. Finish strong!

TINA BLACK

Do you have the heart of a finisher?

What are your top three goals this year, to have your best year ever?

How will you make certain to finish strong?

In Week 12, I challenged you to do the platform exercise and repeat it quarterly. It's that time again! Review the platform exercise from Week 12 and update your answers as needed:

1. On a scale of 1–10, how do you rate your life?

2. What would a 10 look like for you?

3. Why do you want your dream?

4. What are you willing to pay, do, or become to live your dream?

5. What are your current opportunities?

6. What are your strengths?

7. Who do you know that can help you?

8. What can you get rid of that no longer serves you?

In one sentence, who or what do you need to become so you can have what you want?

Week 51

Finish Strong!

"Are you going to finish strong?"

— NICK VUJICIC

In the beginning of this book, I challenged you to choose one word for the year rather than making a New Year's resolution, and then I asked you to think about living an uncommon life.

I've developed some questions for you to ponder as we finish this year together and you start to prepare for the coming year. My coach and mentor John Maxwell has taught all of us coaches over the years that he always spends the last few weeks of December looking back over his year and remembering his successes and failures so he can prepare his heart for the coming year. That's probably some of the best advice I've ever heard.

So here's my challenge to you: take the rest of this month to ask yourself these questions ...

What were some of your victories?

What were some of your failures?

What could you do more of?

What could you do less of?

I challenge you to look over these questions, take some time to answer them, and take time to prepare yourself for the coming year.

TINA BLACK

What were some of your victories?

What were some of your failures?

What could you do more of?

What could you do less of?

Week 52

Circumstances Reveal Where Your Hope Lives

"Adversity does not build character, it reveals it."

— JAMES LANE ALLEN

I heard a message from pastor and author Mark Wargo that really inspired this final leadership message: adversity reveals character, and your character alone determines what kind of leader you will be.

Each year brings a lot of highs and lows for me, and I suspect the same is true for you.

In one recent year, I received some news that really challenged me to remember where my hope lives: health news, financial news, the news about the Paris and Orlando attacks, and the news about the police massacre in Texas, to name a few. I'm a woman of faith so I apologize if this offends you, but my hope is in God alone. It's not in my business, my marriage, my family, my business partners, or the government. My hope is in God.

How about you? Have you been challenged with some less-than-desirable circumstances? Have you lost your faith in God? Your passion? Have you lost hope?

I want to tell you that hope is here. Nothing is impossible for God.

So here's my challenge. Seek God. Don't listen to me. Don't listen to people. Just sit alone and ask God to give you hope. Go ahead. Try it. And remember … circumstances reveal where your hope lives. I hope it will be in God.

TINA BLACK

My mentor Kelly Cardenas once challenged me to set the timer for 1 minute, stare at one spot, and ask myself, "What is my purpose?"

That's your challenge today. Set your timer for 1 minute and ask yourself, "What is my purpose?" Write it here.

CPSIA information can be obtained
at www.ICGtesting.com
Printed in the USA
BVOW08s0853280417
482340BV00005B/7/P

9 781943 127511